# HIDDEN TREASURE

Women Translating Women
A collaborative project of the Ashoka Centre for Translation, the Susham Bedi Memorial Fund and Zubaan Publishers

The Ashoka Centre for Translation, through its initiatives, is committed to thinking about translation from a many-to-many perspective to foster India's multilingual ethos. The Women Translating Women project, under which this book has been supported, is a joint initiative of the Centre and the Susham Bedi Memorial Fund. The Fund, established in memory of the Hindi poet and author Susham Bedi (1 July 1945–20 March 2020), supports the publication of 12 books over two years by Zubaan Publishers.

translation.ashoka.edu.in
sushambedi.com
zubaanbooks.com

# HIDDEN TREASURE

*Sangeeta Bandyopadhyay*
*Translated by Ipsa S*

zubaan

ZUBAAN
128 B Shahpur Jat, 1st floor
NEW DELHI 110 049
Email: contact@zubaanbooks.com
Website: www.zubaanbooks.com

First published by Zubaan Publishers Pvt. Ltd 2024



10 9 8 7 6 5 4 3 2 1

ISBN 978 81 94253 34 1 (paperback)
ISBN 978 81 94253 36 5 (ebook)

Zubaan is an independent feminist publishing house based in New Delhi with a strong academic and general list. It was set up as an imprint of India's first feminist publishing house, Kali for Women, and carries forward Kali's tradition of publishing world quality books to high editorial and production standards. *Zubaan* means tongue, voice, language, speech in Hindustani. Zubaan publishes in the areas of the humanities, social sciences, as well as in fiction, general non-fiction, and books for children and young adults under its Young Zubaan imprint.

Typeset in Sabon 11/16.
Printed and bound at Chaman Offset.

# Hidden Treasure

# 1

The space under the huge bed propped up even higher by bricks was Chintamoni's storage room. Not because the kitchen didn't have enough space. The kitchen was in fact quite large, but mice and mole-rats as big as cats were always scurrying in and out of the drain hole. Besides, the water vat in the kitchen was where she stored wood, coal, and dry cow dung. A jagged stone used for breaking coal lay on the floor. There was also a hammer that had a piece of wood jammed above its wobbly handle to hold it steady. Apart from this, the kitchen housed coal in bamboo baskets and a pile of old, broken items. Kerosene tins and other belongings were usually also strewn over the coal heap.

Chintamoni found it impossible to discard even the oldest and dirtiest of things.

One couldn't really call Chintamoni filthy, untidy, or lazy. But people were quite indifferent to sanitation and hygiene in the times I'm writing about.

In those days, the people of Kolkata would wash their clothes in the same place where they urinated. In the older parts of the city, you could end up stepping on shit if you were even slightly absent-minded. Most neighbourhoods had uncovered drains. People of all ages habitually squatted by them and took care of their morning business. In front of each house was a small pile of garbage. People disposed of their rubbish casually on the street, so listening to cats, dogs, and crows fighting over leftovers all day long had become a routine occurrence. A wild commotion would arise if a crow stole fish bones from one house and perched on fresh clothes on a clothesline in some other house. Crows were treated with great disgust in the homes of Brahmin widows. If a crow sat on fresh clothes, they had to be washed all over again. Back then it was quite common for women to exclaim, 'Oh, my wretched luck!' at the slightest inconvenience.

In those days, fights broke out regularly between dogs and humans over discarded leftovers. You often came upon this scene in the narrow lanes of Kolkata's middle-class neighbourhoods. A gaunt figure would be crouching down and hunting through the trash for food while dogs closed in on him from all sides. The dogs would howl while the man grimaced energetically at them and swung a stick around his head, swearing colourfully. The dogs would retreat and approach again, teeth bared.

The old houses had odd layouts. Entering through the front door, you went into a courtyard. It was surrounded by an elevated ledge ringed with rooms all around. In most houses, the handpump and bathroom were outside, so residents were bound to get drenched on the way to using them on rainy days. This was also why the floor was always covered in wet, muddy tracks. Housework was usually done with water stored for that very purpose. The floor of the kitchen was perpetually flooded. Housewives usually wiped their wet hands on their saris, leaving them sodden from breast to belly. The end of a sari was used for almost every purpose imaginable. Women used it to wipe their sweat and then their tears. Then they wiped their noses with it, and used it to lift hot pots off the stove to prevent their hands from being scalded. It was used to wipe a plate before serving food on it. It always proved useful for wiping their children's noses. Children quite often had snot running down their faces back then.

Several rules and laws had been laid down in ancient times to teach humans about cleanliness and sanctity and to lead a lifestyle of superior quality. But just as original pronunciations of words deteriorate into colloquial versions, these ancient laws had evolved into completely illogical yet universal and sacrosanct customs.

In the times I'm writing about, widows often caused a great nuisance just to retain their command over the household. In north Kolkata, one family had grown fed up with the behaviour of their widowed mother. Fresh water from Tala Tank always ran from their taps, but the widow flat out refused to drink it. She stubbornly insisted that the water used for her cooking be brought from the Ganga. Every month, 10 rickshaws went to Bagbazar Ghat to bring back 20 pitchers of water for her. The water had to be fetched the day before Ekadoshi—any later than that and the water of the Ganga would turn salty, bringing tiny, ant-like crabs with it. One room in their house had been set aside just to store these pitchers. Once the water settled in the pots, a thick layer of mud collected at the bottom. The widow drank the clean water that remained on top. She used it for cooking and sprinkled it outside every door in the mornings and evenings. The mud from the bottom was used for scrubbing dishes.

Chintamoni's mother-in-law had been very fastidious as well. She used to love drinking tea, but only when there was jaggery in it. Although a widow in a Kayastha family, her customs and values were as rigid as a Brahmin's. She'd passed on this exhaustive set of values to Chintamoni, and recited them all the time, even after being confined to bed. Chintamoni continued following these rules long after her mother-in-law's death. But the gulf between proper sanitation and orthodox values had left its mark on her domestic life.

Naturally, the vat for storing cow dung and coal drew a constant stream of cockroaches, ticks, and lizards to the kitchen. Back then, people had no qualms about sharing their living space with these pests. Chintamoni kept her box of spices, salt container, and kitchen utensils on a broken bench in the kitchen. In the larger and darker of their two rented rooms, she stored rice sacks, tins of pulses, and grain baskets under the bed, and used an old coconut oil tin to measure out the rice and pulses. The other room, which was a bit more suitable to live in, was the bedroom. Its window was covered with wire netting—the curtains had been made by cutting up a sari. There was a trunk for clothes, a wooden chest, and stools to sit on during mealtimes. Biscuit tins were stored under the raised bed. There were also milk pots, jars of sweets or pickles, and tins for muri and other food. Boxes of shondesh were always kept under a large brass bowl. During winter, a space was cleared under the bed for storing liquid jaggery. A wooden cupboard with a mirror, a wall rack, two tin chairs, and two wooden chairs were the only other pieces of furniture in the room. There was a linen rug on the floor. Chintamoni's children, Sumantra and Sharbari, would sit on it to study or to play ludo and bagatelle.

Chintamoni's elder daughter Urmila had been married off to a financially stable young man from a Bhattacharya family in Shibpur as soon as she'd turned 19. The Bhattacharyas were quite wealthy. Only a year had passed since her marriage, but Urmila displayed no attachment to her own family. She was living in great luxury. Sometimes she'd send a letter—it was usually shorter than a full page.

Chintamoni's younger daughter Sharbari was 16. She'd failed her exams twice and was now in Class Eight. Sumantra was the most beloved and precious of Chintamoni's children. He was a diligent student and scored the highest marks in math and English. But a hole in the 10-year-old boy's heart had left Chintamoni's lower-middle-class family in constant distress. The anxiety never ended. Manmatha had told Chintamoni that if this child didn't survive, they could try to have another son. Chintamoni had agreed. For now, they'd decided to have no more children.

Manmatha didn't have to search very hard to find a groom for Urmila. They'd selected the very first candidate. Once the groom's family had inspected Urmila, they made no fuss about dowry. The blessing ceremony for the couple was performed on the spot. Urmila was married the next month. A fortunate daughter from a poor family, Urmila had inherited her beauty from her mother. Although her father was a poor man living in meagre, rented rooms, Urmila behaved like the girls from wealthy families. Her gait, speech, expressions, and love for admiring herself in the mirror had convinced her family that she must be married to a wealthy man, or she would take her life. In the end, Urmila's vanity won out.

But Chintamoni surpassed Urmila in her beauty. She was both tall and slim, but not slim enough for her collarbones to show. Not a single bone or rib stuck out on her slender figure. Her back was fleshy; her belly had a healthy swell to it. Her hands and feet were impeccable. She had fair, moist skin. To describe her in more detail, one could say Chintamoni had large breasts which sagged just a bit. What lay beneath her sari was enticing. There was no feminine bulge between her waist and hip—instead, the stretch of skin there was quite taut. Just as drawers keep sliding down the flat waists of schoolgirls, Chintamoni too had to fasten her petticoat very tightly to stop it from sliding off. Yet, even this flaw looked appealing on her, as though her skin were made of butter that had naturally melted in places.

Chintamoni's hair cascaded down past her waist. She was slightly snub-nosed with thin lips and large eyes. When she wore a sindoor bindi, one couldn't help staring at her. Considering her alluring appearance, it was a wonder that she had ended up with a man as unimpressive and mediocre as Manmatha. His uncle had told her family he was a student of law. Needless to say, this was a complete lie. Chintamoni deeply regretted her marriage. Her heart was starved of several unfulfilled desires. But she'd slowly come to accept her fate and everything it held, from her mother-in-law's fastidiousness and having to wipe her clean in her last days to the ticks and mice that infested the house. She'd even accepted having to recycle old saris over and over till they were tattered. But she hadn't managed to accept living with Manmatha Ghosh. One could clearly see that Chintamoni hated her husband. But Manmatha thought Chintamoni loved him dearly.

It wasn't long after Urmila's marriage that an astrologer came to the house in a red dhoti with several strings of rudraksha beads draped around his neck. They were told he was a worshipper of the goddess Mahakali. His name was Kalishankar. He was given lodging in the room on the terrace of the second floor.

A road snaked through the neighbourhood of Haldarpara in Kalighat, ending in front of the Kali temple. Kalachand Haldar's house stood at that very spot. It was over a century old and bore a derelict appearance. Once, the Haldar home had been quite lively. Back then, they'd owned a factory at the mouth of Kalighat Bridge that manufactured wooden furniture. They also had a showroom for furniture in the business district. They had several shops, including one for saris, in Bhabanipur Market. The male line of the family had descended from the original priests of Kalighat Temple. On a few rare occasions they still received commissions to conduct pujas. Over the last 100 years, Kalachand Haldar's descendants had moved away. At present, the house was jointly owned by four members of the family.

Two of them occupied seven or eight rooms on the first floor. The other two brothers had rented out three rooms on the ground floor a very long time ago and moved elsewhere. Chintamoni's family was one of those three tenants.

Balai Haldar owned some of the rooms on the first floor. His mother Rajeshwari was a very religious and domineering widow. Kalishankar was allowed to stay in the house on her orders. She also arranged for him to be provided with two meals. Kalishankar was seldom glimpsed outside his terrace room, except when he came downstairs to buy bidis. The doors of his room were usually shut. Sometimes, he was seen pacing around the veranda on the terrace.

Kalishankar was served his meals by Sanaka, the Brahmin girl who cooked for Balai Haldar's family. She often said with a frown, 'Who knows what sort of Kali worshipper that man is. I haven't seen a single picture of Ma Kali in his room. Just bidi stubs all over the floor. When I asked him, "Why don't you sweep the floor?" he just glared at me! God knows why Ma is looking after this crook.'

Chintamoni had been suspicious of Kalishankar from the first time she'd seen him. He had bright eyes but countless wrinkles running across his forehead. What worries could a pilgrim devotee possibly have? She'd thought, *Well, why should I bother? Since they're giving him shelter, he's their responsibility.*

Ever since Kalishankar's arrival, several people, including the Haldars' relatives, had gone to him to get their fortunes read. The exciting prospect of a palm reading in their humdrum, middle-class lives had drawn several people to the house. The man had looked at Rajeshwari's palm and immediately said that her first son Nemai had gone missing at nine. The old woman sobbed and asked, 'Is he alive?'

'He is. Search towards the north.'

That's how everything began. Kalishankar read the palm of Rajeshwari's nephew's wife. He advised them to buy a lottery ticket. It was the only way their luck would return. His advice was followed obediently. They spent a whole five rupees on a ticket and won 120 rupees straightaway. The accuracy of his predictions left everyone amazed. Greatly delighted, Rajeshwari organised a Mangalchandi puja and generously distributed batasha and goja. Chintamoni wasn't allowed to enter the ceremonial room. She called her children and stooped to gather the batasha that had spilled across the door.

# 2

Kalishankar told Parimal, one of the tenants, 'Get into iron trading, it will bring you much wealth!' But Parimal worked at the municipal corporation, where he made birth and death certificates. How could he begin trading iron all of a sudden? Nonetheless, the advice lingered in his head. He found a house that was being torn down and bought iron beams, railings, and window grills from the site. Parimal swiftly earned 200 rupees after selling them to someone in Ekbalpur. Afterwards, he would sign in at his job with the corporation and then roam the city looking for houses being knocked down. He began to make handsome profits after a few months of persistent work.

Kalishankar read Chintamoni's palm as well. He said that the sea posed a threat to her life but didn't predict much else. Manmatha heard the reading and sighed heavily. 'I'd been thinking of going on a holiday in Puri. Better not go anymore.' Chintamoni didn't know whether to laugh or cry. 'This poor household will fall apart if something happens to you, Chinu!'

Manmatha had never taken Chintamoni on holiday besides visiting her parents' house in Krishnanagar for Jamai Shoshti. They hadn't been anywhere in 20 years.

But more important than the reading was how Kalishankar's hand had trembled curiously when he held her palm. Chintamoni had noticed it. His touch sent a bolt of lightning tingling through her 37-year-old voluptuous body. Rajeshwari was a strict believer in caste. She was the landlord and belonged to a family of Brahmins, while Chintamoni was a Kayastha. So Chintamoni was made to sit on a mat on the floor, while Kalishankar sat on Rajeshwari's bed. At one point, Kalishankar's foot deliberately brushed against Chintamoni's knee.

Several people came to get their palms read that evening. Chintamoni returned to her kitchen and started making rotis. They turned out inedible, and a few even burned. After that day, a peculiar change came over her usually practical nature. Day and night, Kalishankar clung to her thoughts like a shadow.

One afternoon, Chintamoni was scrubbing her feet in the bathroom with a stone when she happened to glance upwards and saw Kalishankar standing on the terrace. She started, as though she had seen a ghost. There was a gap of about six inches between the top of the tin door and the roof of the bathroom. It was usually covered with a sheet. The owners of the house had never bothered to look into it, so it had never been fixed. The sheet had flown away and landed on the roof of the bathroom—Chintamoni hadn't noticed. When she saw Kalishankar, she hastily wrapped her wet petticoat tighter around herself, thinking, *the nerve of this man! Imagine peeping on a married woman bathing. So shameless, he isn't even leaving!*

Then she changed her mind. She remembered the slight trembling of his hand and the unspoken message in it. She remembered his foot brushing against her knee. Chintamoni didn't reach out to lower the sheet. She began to bathe slowly with the petticoat still wrapped around herself. She scrubbed her limbs with soap and rose to her feet. She was sure her petticoat would slide off now. She drew the curtain, then shifted it slightly and saw that Kalishankar had grown excited on the terrace. He was impatiently waiting for the curtain to be drawn aside again.

A blazing desire was spreading through Chintamoni's body. Breathing rapidly, she began to pour water over herself.

The house was always full of people. The daily commotion started at dawn and died down abruptly around two in the afternoon. Sharbari and Sumantra left for school early in the morning. Around 10, Manmatha also left for work. Chintamoni usually had lunch by one o'clock and took a nap after glancing through the newspapers. But from that day, Chintamoni's monotonous life took a complete turn. The game in the bathroom seized her like an addiction. The next day, she went for her bath after two o'clock, removing the sheet in one swift motion as she entered. Then she turned and glanced at the terrace. Yes, Kalishankar was standing there. Had she been a young girl, she would have started giggling right then. But Chintamoni, the mother of three children, just stared fiercely back at him. A ruthless desire had been tormenting her since yesterday. She'd have no peace till she quenched it. She began to pour mugs of water over herself, still dressed in her sari, blouse, and petticoat. Kalishankar looked like he wanted to jump down from the terrace and wrestle her to the ground right there in the backyard. Chintamoni began playing, pretending to be oblivious. She removed her blouse but covered her chest with the end of her sari. Then she dropped the sari but covered her breasts with her long hair. She turned around, her bare back facing Kalishankar, and started rubbing soap over her chest. Then suddenly she turned to face him and stood still, her heavy breasts fully exposed. It seemed like Kalishankar was about to fall over the railing and tumble off the roof like a dry leaf.

Chintamoni kept playing for a long time. Finally, she dropped all her clothes and sat down on the edge of the tub, torn about what to do next. Kalishankar's movements seemed to indicate that he was trying to restrain himself. If they hadn't been afraid of being discovered, their maddened lovemaking might have demolished the room on the roof by now!

They couldn't escape the fear of being humiliated. But any shame, hesitation, or restraint between them seemed to have melted away. Each knew what the other wanted without ever having spoken about it. People were always going to the roof for some reason or the other. Only in the afternoon did the two of them get an opportunity.

About three or four days later, Chintamoni proceeded to the roof in the afternoon with a pile of wet clothes. No matter how quietly she tried to climb the stairs, the metal banister always vibrated and made a sound. Just when she'd reached the second floor, someone knocked on the front door. Startled, Chintamoni hurried downstairs. Someone called out from upstairs, 'Who is it?' The postman often came to the house around this time. Since there were only women in the house in the afternoons, the front door was locked. When Chintamoni hurriedly opened the door, there was no one but Manmatha outside. He was sweating and looked exhausted.

'Oh, it's you. What's the matter?' Chintamoni was surprised but annoyed too.

'I'm feeling very sick today, Chinu. My boss asked me to go home. I'll lie down for a bit. Come and sit next to me?'

Chintamoni hung the wet clothes out in the courtyard and got busy tending to Manmatha. Frustrated, she said, 'My cursed luck! I must have done something bad in my past life. That's why fate keeps deceiving me.' Manmatha Ghosh thought his wife's lamentations were out of concern for his health. He drank the sharbat of salt, sugar, and lemon she brought him and said, 'Don't worry, Chinu. I feel better now. I just need some rest. Commuting on buses and trams is wearing me out!'

Manmatha stayed home another day and then went back to work. That day Chintamoni tried to go to the roof again with some wet clothes. As soon as she reached the second floor, Rajeshwari called out from her room, 'Who is it? Is that you, Chinu?'

Chintamoni quietly walked to her room and stood by the door. 'Yes, Mashima.'

'Going to the roof?'

'Yes, to hang the clothes out to dry,' she said nervously.

'All right, come sit with me when you're done. I can't sleep. Come chat with me.'

'All right.'

Thinking it would look suspicious if she didn't go to the roof, Chintamoni went up the stairs anyway. But there was no way to carry out her plan. It would be a disaster if Kalishankar were to pounce on her. Rajeshwari would suspect something if she took too long to return. A stranger—especially a man—lived on the roof now.

It wouldn't do for young girls and married women to roam about there.

Chintamoni reached the roof. The door of Kalishankar's room swung open soundlessly at once. Placing both his hands on the doorframe, the man retreated slightly into his room. It faced the north and had begun to grow dark by then. Chintamoni stood still, her insides quaking with fear, excitement, and impatience. Her chest began to heave provocatively. She looked at Kalishankar's face properly, standing close to him for the first time. When she saw him, desire—and even a hint of love—flared up within her. Suddenly, she felt very embarrassed about her shameless little game in the bathroom. Kalishankar gestured at her to come towards him. She shook her head, her heart pounding. Her ears began to heat up. My god, how immoral this man must think she was! But that wasn't true. Her youth had nearly faded. She spent her days counting every rupee—Manmatha never gave her any money. Fear for her son was always troubling her. Sometimes he struggled just to breathe, and her heart thrashed with motherly distress. They didn't even have enough money to take him to a good doctor. But Kalishankar's heated gaze had stirred her dormant desires. Her repressed frustration at Manmatha had only fuelled her decision to cheat on him. But that didn't mean she was some kind of adulteress.

Chintamoni tried to look grave. Faintly, she said, 'No.' With shaking hands, she hung the two saris on a clothesline and retreated a few steps. Suddenly, Kalishankar rushed into his room. When he returned, it was with something in his hands. Kalishankar approached her. 'Oh god!' Chintamoni gasped in terror. In a flash, Kalishankar grasped her right arm, on which she wore the bangles from her wedding, and said, 'Come here!'

Chintamoni shook her head violently, saying, 'No... Mashima is awake!' She saw that Kalishankar was holding a thick 24-inch gold necklace. He forcefully pulled her into his arms and began to rub his face against her neck. Chintamoni tried to throw him off. Suddenly, Kalishankar put the necklace around her neck and whispered, 'I have more, I can give you more!'

Finally managing to free herself, Chintamoni hurried downstairs and immediately hid the necklace inside her blouse. It was so heavy that she thought it would fall out of the loose, frayed garment. Instead of going to Rajeshwari's room, Chintamoni went directly to her own and closed the door. For some time, she lay panting on her bed. The necklace lying on the bed seemed like a glittering snake. She stared at it fearfully and then reached for it. Then she tossed and turned on the bed and drove herself to misery, wondering where to hide it.

# 3

Chintamoni filled her idle hours with sighs. How strange human nature was. No pain, no gain. But she shouldn't think such things. If something were to happen to Manmatha, they'd have no choice but to beg on the streets. She rose from the bed and glanced at the kitchen. The jewellery had become a great source of relief for her. She'd never locked the kitchen before—it had been enough to put the security chain in place. But now she just couldn't rest easy until she had locked it. What would she do, where would she keep them? If only she could get some more jewellery from that box! But as expected, he hadn't bothered to give her any more. She sat bolt upright in bed. She would snatch it all from him. No, that wouldn't be possible. There was only one way.

But thinking of this option made her change her mind again. The man was ravenous. He was just impossible.

Never had her breasts endured such torment. It seemed as if Kalishankar had been fasting since the beginning of time. Barely had they finished once when he'd lunged at her for a second round. She'd managed to escape before he tried a third time. Chintamoni had begun to hide the bites and bruises on her body from Manmatha. But there was nothing she could do about the way the man tormented her heart. Who knew what fate held for her.

A chance came her way once more. That day Chintamoni received two more pieces of jewellery—a nose ring inlaid with pearl and a velvet choker with a lotus centrepiece threaded through with gold. Then there was yet another opportunity. One day, both the families living on the first floor left to attend a relative's wedding in Chandannagar for three days. Sanaka too took three days' leave to go home to her village. Before leaving, Rajeshwari told Chintamoni, 'Chinu, listen, we won't be home for three days. Sanaka won't be coming either. No one will be cooking. Can you give Kalishankar his meals? Otherwise I'll have to find some other way.'

Chintamoni said, 'Why not, Mashima? I don't mind. Two more servings of rice won't cost much.'

'Put his rice and dal in separate bowls and take his plate to the room. Send Manmatha at night.'

'Yes of course, Mashima, don't worry about that. But we are Kayasthas, do you think he'll eat our food?' Chintamoni asked, laughing.

'I asked him. Kalishankar said, "I've lived in crematoriums and eaten off plates meant for the dead. I don't believe in caste. Everything is Ma's prasad after all."'

'Such talk scares me, Mashima. Sumantra and Sharbari are frightened of him anyway. All this talk of crematoriums makes me tremble.'

Rajeshwari beamed. 'Ma herself is a figure of terror, Chinu. She wears a garland of heads, she's always got ghosts and witches around her. Still she defeats all evil and reigns fearlessly. All my life I've prayed to her for anything I need.'

Chintamoni thought to herself, *Hmph! It was luck that got her married into this family. That's how she's spent her life in such comfort. She doesn't have an ounce of beauty. That scaly brown skin and thin hair—yet look at her luck! Her sons and daughters-in-law live under her thumb. Her grandchildren are always following her around. They send for a doctor over the smallest sneeze. Her husband was still alive when I came here, and what a henpecked man he was! The whole neighbourhood sneered at him. Not to his face, of course.*

Rajeshwari said, 'I read the *Kathamrita*. It just calms my mind. Whenever something troubles me, I think of Ramakrishna Paramahansa, Chinu. I have no interest in domestic life now. I've told my sons and daughters-in-law to keep me out of things. Inform me of births. Don't inform me of deaths. But who can stop news of death, after all?'

'I really want to read the *Kathamrita* too. I've asked Urmila's father to bring one for me.'

'Oh yes, read it if you can, your heart will feel full. Ramakrishna, Vivekananda, Vidyasagar—they were all great men. They will never be reborn, and none like them will be born again.'

'But can anyone become a Ramakrishna or a Vivekananda just because they want to? After all, those great men were born wise from their mothers' wombs, weren't they?'

Chintamoni was in the mood for a deep conversation.

Rajeshwari shook her head. 'But what good could Vivekananda do if he were reborn in our times?'

'Why, Mashima?'

'Widows are getting remarried at will these days. My own uncle's granddaughter got married, then became a widow and got her husband's job. Then out of nowhere she got married to her husband's cousin after having an affair. I heard that she was even pregnant by then.'

As Chintamoni listened, she stepped over the doorframe and entered Rajeshwari's room. Pressing the end of her sari to her mouth as though she'd never heard of such domestic scandals before, she said, 'Really?'

'And do you know what Ananya did?'

'Ananya? Which Ananya?'

'There's this distant cousin, her son's wife. She's about your age. Her husband died two years ago, and she got his job. She and her mother-in-law were living together happily. But now she's going to marry a colleague and be part of a new family. Hmph! You'd think she'd look after her mother-in-law, who faced so many hardships in bringing her son up, but no. How do they do it, Chinu? How can she even think of sleeping in the same bed with another man so soon after her husband's death?'

'Times have changed.'

'But then again, how long should widows go about grieving and looking mournful, especially the young ones? What a life widows have. Can't eat most things, not allowed at celebrations. Maybe it's all right for widows to get married again. But what about divorce? It's everywhere! And women are having affairs with men despite having husbands of their own. Sins in every family.'

Chintamoni had been thinking of sitting down, but now she began to back away. Once Rajeshwari started there was no stopping her. 'Who knows what else I'll have to see in this life! Shoshti Haldar's house is beside Nakuleshwar Mandir—I've heard his nephew's wife is having an affair with the man who buys their groceries. They found the love letters. Is this how a girl with a graduate degree is supposed to behave? You know where Moushumi and her family live, the house at the corner? The mother and the daughter both wear sleeveless blouses. Her mother goes to the cinema with a man, and the girl goes with the same man to Babughat on his motorbike, arms wrapped around him and all. Disgusting!'

'How did you know they go to Babughat?'

'Chinu, do you think my ears and eyes are closed to the world? I could sit in this room all day and still know everything that happens. I can see everything, do you understand?'

Chintamoni went downstairs looking rather downcast.

However, those three days went quite well for her. The second floor was empty—Parimal and Tapanbabu's families on the first floor were busy with their own affairs. Chintamoni went up to the roof several times a day, but no one noticed. Manmatha even chatted with Kalishankar when he delivered his food at night. Chintamoni cooked and laid out Kalishankar's meal without fail. Sometimes shaak, sometimes kasundi, once she'd even sent him fish head curry. She also made some payesh one day. She discovered in those three days that the lure of desire was no less than the lure of money! Even as a mother of three, Chintamoni had never realised this before. As soon as she went to the roof, they came together like a pair of breeding rabbits. Their union was unbounded, their appetite unending. The well of desire filled up no sooner than it emptied itself.

After one round, Kalishankar grew restless for another. Then Chintamoni smoothened her clothes, went towards the door, and spoke to him in a low voice.

She stayed alert to make sure no one came upon them suddenly. Namita Bou-di had arthritis in her knees, and her mother-in-law was bedridden. Only Parimal's wife Mallika could possibly discover them. Kalishankar would gesture at her again even as she was speaking. The man stayed locked in his room with his stolen goods. He neither went out nor talked to anyone. He was hounded by his fear of the police. Worshipping, reciting mantras—all of it was an act. Only to Chintamoni did he speak frankly. Chintamoni's body was where Kalishankar found all his freedom. One had to give it to Chintamoni—she'd managed to wheedle many secrets out of him. The man had made her his partner in sin. They had been discussing how to sell the jewellery but hadn't found a solution.

'How will I sell the gold? I'll get caught,' Chintamoni said.

A huge neem tree stood in the building's compound. Its shade cooled the room on the roof. Kalishankar would sit there lost in his thoughts, lighting one bidi after another. He scratched his beard and said, 'Will you make panta bhat for me one day?'

'Panta? We don't eat panta bhat. All right, I'll soak some rice in water later. Poor thing! You have so much gold but you can't even make money from it.'

'A man will come during the Durga Pujo days. He'll take the goods and give me money. Once I get it I'll go away to Assam.'

Chintamoni glared at him. 'No!'

She had reason to be angry. If Kalishankar left, she'd remain Manmatha Ghosh's housekeeper forever. But her heart had grown so detached from him. When Manmatha asked her to come to his room at night, she pretended to be sleepy. 'Uff, I'm old now. I don't like these things anymore!'

She felt repelled when Manmatha touched her. Like she was touching a disgusting wet rag. He put powder on his neck and shoulders. He kept a folded handkerchief inside his collar—apparently it made clothes last longer and kept the collar from fraying. But on Kalishankar's body was the scent of depravity, of sin, of tobacco and sweat and money that mingled together to bewitch Chintamoni.

Kalishankar gave her a suspicious look. 'What do you mean, no? I must go! Should I just sit here waiting to get caught?'

Chintamoni fumed. 'So you intend to run away after exploiting me? No, that cannot be.'

Kalishankar rocked back and forth. 'What do you mean exploit? You came to me of your own free will. What will you do to me? You're the one who'll end up in danger if you do something. And have I deprived you? You've taken whatever you pleased from the box. No one's recorded how much.'

'Everything in this room is unrecorded, Kalishankar!' Chintamoni burst out. Her own tone surprised her.

Kalishankar's eyes widened. 'I don't like your tone.'

Suddenly Chintamoni burst into tears. 'You're the one who tempted me. How else would I have known about all this wealth? But I don't want your jewellery. I was hurt deeply when you said you'd go away. Has no one ever loved you?'

'Love! I have no mother or father. I was an orphan, sweeping the floor of the Kali Mandir and helping with the rituals. Do you understand? I had faith in my heart, that's why I found a mother.'

'You've seen Ma Kali for yourself?'

'Of course! Ma was the one who told me, run, run away with these jewels! What use do I have for them? They'll lie rotting in the safe for decades. Break the safe, donate them, meditate, open an orphanage. Don't stay in the temple!'

Chintamoni started laughing at him. Then she said, 'Don't go, please don't go. Will we ever meet again if you leave?'

A couple of months later, with only two weeks to go for Durga Pujo, a fierce quarrel broke out one morning between Parimal and his wife. Parimal was about to leave for work, after both their daughters had gone to college. Usually Mallika would dress up and go to the cinema as soon as Parimal had left. She loved watching films. Ever since Parimal's income had gone up, she'd begun flaunting new desires and fancies. For example, she'd gone to New Market a few days ago and bought an expensive set of cups and plates. She couldn't bear to keep serving guests tea in discoloured, chipped cups when they visited after Bijoya. Today she was going to take her bath after Parimal left, and had just served him his meal—rice, boiled potatoes, fried lady's finger, and fish curry.

'Is this all there is to eat?' Parimal screamed.

'What else do you expect? You'll have to make do with this. Didi will be here any moment, I need to get ready.'

'God, you're always going to the cinema!'

'Why do you care?'

'Look at these tiny pieces of vegetable! Couldn't you add some onions to the aloo sheddho? Why haven't you made any daal?'

'There's no daal at home, we need to buy some.'

'Moog, chhola, khyashari—is there nothing at all?'

'How am I supposed to make daal with chhola? They need to be soaked in advance, don't they? I told you to get me one of those new pressure cookers.'

'It's very easy to make demands, but it needs money!'

'Then get some.'

'How much more? I slave like a dog already! We have to marry off our two daughters as well. They aren't as pretty as Urmila. You think we can get them out the door without a dowry?'

'Look, their daughter might be pretty, but my girls are beautiful to me. Besides, they're in college, education has its own benefits. They can work and earn for themselves.'

'Why should they have to work?'

'Why not? Are they the daughters of some grand zamindar or something?'

Chintamoni poured some of the biuli daal she had made with mouri and hing into a bowl, walked into their room, and put it down next to Parimal's plate. 'Here, Thakurpo,' she said.

Mallika was in a hurry, so she didn't try arguing further. She took her soap case, towel, mug, and bucket and went to the bathroom.

She was dressed in a black and red sari with a floral print. She'd covered her hair bun with a net. Before leaving, she put a piece of paan in her mouth. After locking both rooms, she went to give Chintamoni her keys. Chintamoni was sitting on the rug and sewing buttons onto Sumantra's shirt. Mallika handed her the keys and said, 'You didn't mind us talking about you then, did you?'

'No,' said Chintamoni. 'Thakurpo says things like that all the time!'

'But tell me, why does he say such things? Are my daughters ugly?'

'Is there any use paying attention to the things he says?'

Mallika's sister was on her way in a rickshaw. Mallika would leave as soon as she arrived. Her ears were pricked for sounds near the front door. 'You should have come with us too,' she told Chintamoni. 'You used to go out before, to the cinema or the theatre. Nowadays you don't go even when I ask you. You're stuck in your room all day. There are signs of worry on your face. Has something happened? Are you having another child or something?'

Chintamoni smiled wanly. 'What are you saying, Mallika? Nothing of the sort!'

'What is it then?'

Mallika's sister opened the front door and peeped in at that very moment. 'I'll see you later,' said Mallika and left.

Chintamoni heaved a sigh of relief. She avoided most conversations these days. Who knew what she might let slip. As for reasons to worry, distress and financial crises had been their companions for a long time. Frustration, sorrow, and rage always churned within her. But this rage was Chintamoni's fuel. The crash and bang of utensils, rebukes, and muttered complaints filled her domestic life. She'd always had despair in her heart for Sumantra, but never any mental disorder. Everything had changed now though. Some kind of mental illness had crept up within her. There was no cure for it. She found no urge to do anything except hoard more gold. She feared nothing but the possibility of Kalishankar leaving. There was an emptiness she could sense inside her. If she could go to Kalishankar just once, she would sob her heart out to him.

As she worked a new thread through her needle, she heard the metal ring on the front door being rattled faintly. Chintamoni got up to open the door. A short man in a shirt and dhoti stood in front of her. 'Does someone named Kalishankar live here? I'm a distant cousin of his. I've come to see him!'

Chintamoni realised that the man they'd been expecting had arrived. For a fleeting moment she considered telling him no one of that name lived here. Then she wondered why the man would believe her. He must have known already. Instead, he'd wonder why a middle-class married woman would want to hide Kalishankar's presence. If he found out Chintamoni had a large portion of Kalishankar's loot, he wouldn't be pleased at all. She would be in great danger. If Kalishankar told him everything, she'd have no choice. She was willing to return the jewellery if it came to that. In any case, this hidden treasure hadn't been of any use to her so far. Chintamoni hadn't managed to muster up the courage to use it.

She said, 'Yes, he's on the second floor. You can go up.'

'Thank you,' said the man, smiling widely. A huge bundle hung over his shoulder, just like the ones Kashmiri shawl-sellers carried. But it didn't seem like there was anything inside it. The man wore leather slippers that seemed brand new, but his feet were cracked and muddy, as if he worked in the fields. Tears came to Chintamoni's eyes. Kalishankar really was leaving! The day had come. The man glanced around the house as he slowly climbed the stairs. Balai Haldar's wife came out on the first-floor balcony at that very moment.

'Who are you?'

'I've come to see Kalishankar. I'm his cousin.'

'Kalishankar's cousin? Really? He never said he had a family. All right, you can go upstairs.'

Chintamoni's heart grew restles. She wanted to go to the roof. But that would look suspicious.

About two hours later, she thought she heard someone washing their hands beside the drain on the first floor. She peeped outside and saw it was the visitor. Perhaps Balai Haldar's family had given him something to eat. Sanaka was standing in front of him. The man said, 'I ate very well. Tell Ma Jononi the food was delicious.'

Then he slowly walked down the stairs and left. Chintamoni noticed that the bundle no longer hung from his shoulder. Where had it gone?

Chintamoni glanced upwards as she entered the bathroom for her bath. No, Kalishankar wasn't standing there with his usual feigned indifference. This was the only time they managed to see each other. Chintamoni no longer played with water while gazing at Kalishankar. Whenever they had a chance they made use of it in the room on the roof. But Kalishankar would still appear at his spot when she went for her bath. Perhaps he was ready to leave now. Right then she decided that she would go up to the roof when the house grew quiet in the afternoon.

Chintamoni couldn't eat any lunch because of the sorrow in her heart. Having waited for the right moment, she finally made her way upstairs. When she reached the roof silently, there was no sign of Kalishankar. She approached his room.

The door had been left wide open. Chintamoni saw that half of Kalishankar's body was hanging off his bed, along with his head and arms. His eyes were wide open, as if they were about to pop out of their sockets. His mouth was open, his face wore a contorted expression. It was clear that Kalishankar was dead.

Chintamoni clapped a hand over her mouth so that she didn't scream. She would have to go downstairs now. She would have to go to the ground floor without letting anyone know. Her knees began to shake. She thought, *God, how far away my room is, it seems a thousand miles!* She felt she'd never get there.

She made it back somehow and collapsed on her bed immediately. She twisted and turned without groaning. Her body began to crumple. That man had killed him. He had murdered him and left. Kalishankar hadn't been able to utter a sound. A murder—god, how frightening! Someone had been killed in the house. A tremendous storm was approaching; would she survive? She was the only one who knew everything. Chintamoni felt her heart grow cold as stone. She fainted. When she came to sometime later, she thought that this sin would never let go of her. It would chase her around. Everyone would find out everything. The newspapers would say, 'Housewife's Affair with Thief, Goddess' Jewellery Recovered!'

People around the world would read the story over and over with relish. She'd be jailed and hanged. Manmatha would kill himself. Urmila would be thrown out of her in-laws' house. Sharbari and Sumantra would beg on the roads. Everything was going to end. Her greed was going to destroy them all. For a few moments, Chintamoni felt like she was losing her mind. She giggled and tore at her hair and sobbed, she slapped herself and banged her head against the bedpost.

Then, suddenly, she calmed down completely. A jug of water was usually kept under the bed—Chintamoni moistened the end of her sari and wiped her eyes with it. Then she waited for the moment when Sanaka's shriek would echo around the house, making her quake.

# 4

Sharbari and Sumantra returned from school around 4.15 or 4.20. When she saw her children, Chintamoni realised she needed to appear calm or people would definitely suspect her. In her efforts to compose herself, she suddenly turned on Sharbari. 'How many times have I told you to wash your own uniform and your brother's when you return from school? You only have two uniforms. Do you like wearing the same sweaty clothes every day? Really, Sharbari, you're 16 years old. Have you seen how much work girls in other houses do? And you? Either you're sewing all day or giggling with older girls in the neighbourhood.'

She finished her diatribe and began to pant. She served her children bananas mashed in chhatu. Then she stood at the window and gossiped with Nipobithi from the next lane, telling her about Urmila. Nipobithi was the matron of a nursing home. She hadn't married and had a sharp tongue. She was almost an old woman now, having spent all her life trying to support her brothers' families. Although she'd never had much to be happy about, she always had a bright smile on her face. Chintamoni felt a searing pain travelling up and down her back as she chatted.

That was when Sanaka's piercing scream made Chintamoni jump—she had to go running to the courtyard. There were no men in the house, only girls and women. Nearly all of them began weeping loudly on hearing Sanaka's description. Chintamoni, too, sent her children into their rooms and went back to the window. 'They're saying Kalishankar is lying dead,' she told Nipobithi, shaking like a leaf. Nipobithi came over with her brothers at once. When Mallika's daughters returned, Chintamoni brought them to her rooms as well. 'Chitra, Mitra, stay here until your mother comes back,' she ordered. The police arrived at the house within an hour.

A man named Kalishankar had been killed. He was about 35. No one knew his real name or identity. He'd been killed by strangulation. A man who had introduced himself as his distant cousin had murdered him and left. The room was in disarray, but they hadn't figured out what the man had been looking for so desperately. The murderer had brought a cloth bundle with him and had left without it. There were only pieces of polystyrene in the bundle, nothing else. The police suspected that the murderer had come to take a box of money or something similar from the man named Kalishankar. They also believed that these men could be linked to the groups smuggling idols of gods—they deduced this from the polystyrene pieces. They searched every nook and cranny of the house for idols or other precious objects but found nothing. Kalishankar must have removed everything from the house much earlier. Balai Haldar, Parimal, Manmatha, Sadhanbabu, and Topenbabu were exhausted from going back and forth to the police station. But the police didn't arrest anyone. Their neighbours came to their rescue and gave witness. Earlier too, Rajeshwari had allowed strangers to board in their house. Nearly everyone knew about her strong belief in palm reading, horoscopes, and all sorts of fortune telling and superstitions. And people didn't stop believing in such things just because they had been tricked by someone they trusted. That was how things were back then. Besides, people used to be generous—they never hesitated to offer shelter to someone who needed it. Several people believed, 'If the gods have given us life, they will surely give us food.' People would always end up in the places where god had ordained they would receive food. This doesn't mean people weren't selfish then. But the people you considered your own included both relatives and neighbours. Their generosity wasn't restricted to their 1,000-square-foot homes like it is today. This was certainly a matter of pride.

All the same, people came to the house and lectured old Rajeshwari. 'Now look what you've done! That lost son of yours will never come back. Just have faith he's happy wherever he is!'

Someone said, 'Once the police are done investigating, get some rituals performed in the house to restore peace, Mashima. It wasn't a natural death—and in a house occupied by Brahmins!'

Some people visited simply to hear frightening stories. People asked Sanaka for her version. Sanaka told them, allowing her imagination to guide the story. 'He would pace up and down on the roof all night, you know, all night,' she said.

But to protect herself she added, 'But yes, he never even looked at women. The house is full of women, but he never teased them or went into their rooms. He didn't have any bad inclinations of that kind.'

No answers were found to the mystery. Gradually, life in the house went back to normal. There was an elaborate ceremony to worship Bipodtarini, the goddess who dispelled danger. Winter arrived and left. Chintamoni participated in discussions and gave her opinion. Sometimes, on idle afternoons, she stared up at the spinning fan in her room, a sob rising in her chest, and thought, *so the man died? He's really dead? The only lover in my life?* Some days, on her way to the bathroom, she looked up at the roof and started, mistakenly thinking someone was standing there. She even began to fear ghosts. Then Balai Haldar rented the room on the roof to a couple of students from Jadavpur University. They were loud and cheerful, spending their time singing, playing the tabla, and quarrelling at the top of their voices. It helped dispel much of the shock of the murder—instead, the house filled with cheer. Rajeshwari died in the month of Chaitra. Urmila came to stay for a few months during her first pregnancy. Sadhan Haldar's daughter was married with much fanfare. Parimal's family bought some land in Jadavpur and left. A newlywed couple, Satyaki and Kakoli, moved into their rooms. The atmosphere of the house changed beyond recognition.

There was just one mystery Chintamoni couldn't get to the bottom of. Where was the remaining jewellery? Where was the jewellery box? It was full of jewellery, and it had to be somewhere in the house. But where? The police had never searched her coal heap—the box must also be lying some place they'd overlooked. Sumantra was very sick the day the police came to search the house. He had a fever of nearly 104 degrees. Chintamoni was crying and looked quite distraught anyway. They'd sent for the doctor, and he'd advised pouring icy water over Sumantra's head until he arrived. Manmatha had brought ice from the ice factory and was breaking it with a pestle in the kitchen when the police came to search the ground floor. They came in, saw Chintamoni and Sumantra, and peeped into the two rooms. They glanced briefly at the kitchen and moved on to Parimal's rooms. Feeling she was safe now, Chintamoni cried with her head on Sumantra's chest. Sumantra told her faintly, 'Ma, don't cry, I'll get better!'

Several months later, Chintamoni was buying a yellow sari in Gariahat Market with Manmatha. As she held it against her skin, she had the thought that she'd got those pieces of jewellery because it was her fate. The other events had only been a means for her destiny to be fulfilled.

There was a large neem tree behind Kalachand Haldar's house which shed fruit whose pulp stained the walls. Nearly 18 or 19 months after Kalishankar's death, on a day of prolonged rainstorms, a leather box fell from the top of the tree with a huge crash. When people peeped out at the noise, they saw several kilos of gold jewellery lying strewn about in Kalachand Haldar's backyard.

Any remaining fear or worry in Chintamoni's heart was completely dispelled by this event. The police came as well and finally solved the mystery. As soon as the jewellery was examined, they knew that it belonged to the idol of a goddess. When they looked up places that had reported the theft of their idol's jewellery, they were led to the robbery of a zamindar's chest in Ballabhpur in Birbhum district. The jewellery was returned. The police assumed that the rest of the stolen goods had been smuggled out by someone else and closed the case.

Chintamoni hadn't shown any signs of abnormal behaviour all this while. One day, she used her own method to weigh the jewellery she had and discovered it was nearly a kilogram of gold. She thought to herself with relish, *When I take it to the jewellery shop, it'll probably turn out to be more, maybe 1 kg and 115 grams. Or a kilogram and a half. Or maybe even 2 kg!* She leaned back happily. These days, she spoke even less than usual. She was always lost in her thoughts, quietly repeating to herself, *I have so much money, so much money.* One day, she locked both rooms and left the house with one gold necklace. She'd decided to take a bus to Bowbazar. She'd go to one of the big shops there and tell them, 'See, this is my grandmother-in-law's necklace, I want to use the gold to make modern jewellery. Tell me how much it weighs after deducting the weight of the impurities. You must calculate your charges for making the new ornaments based on the value of the gold. I won't pay separately.' A new style of pure gold bangles was becoming popular. They were called kucho electric bangles. She thought if she got six of those made, she'd still have some money left over. She'd easily be able to afford treatment for Sumantra with that money. The boy had a fever quite often these days. The doctor had said that he was getting a blood infection repeatedly. How long could things go on this way?

Chintamoni didn't know how to find her away around Bowbazar. She'd been there once or twice to visit a relative, and one other time with Mallika to shop for Durga Pujo. Mallika had bought a sari. Chintamoni hadn't bought anything, she'd only had kulfi malai. Now she walked from the bus stop on Bowbazar Street till she found a shop that seemed nice. It was called Adi Rajlakshmi Jewellers.

Placing the end of her sari in a cowl over her head, she was about to enter the shop when a man popped up in front of her. He said, 'Bouthan, how are you? You've come such a long way all by yourself. Does Dada know? Be careful now, don't get into trouble. Lots of thieves and pickpockets around here. I can be your guard and take you around if you like.'

Drawing back with fear, Chintamoni saw that it wasn't even a full-grown man but an adolescent boy. He was dressed in bell-bottom trousers and a singlet and had several amulets around his neck. Chintamoni had never seen him before. He spoke in a slightly threatening tone. There was a cunning expression on his face, like a wayward, spoilt child's. He was calling her 'Bouthan', he knew she'd come a long way, he was even talking about 'Dada'. Did he know her?

She asked, 'You know who I am?'

The boy laughed horribly. 'I need to know these things, Bouthan. You live in Haldarpara. There was a murder in your house, wasn't there?'

Chintamoni was genuinely terrified. Wiping her eyes with the end of her sari, she wondered what was going on. She hardly ever went out. She doubted too many people in the neighbourhood even knew her. Besides, the boy seemed to be hinting at something else. What she said was, 'I don't have anything valuable. If it gets stolen, so be it. But stealing isn't so easy, the thief can't just run away when it's so crowded. Why don't you do your own work, and I'll do mine. I don't need a guard.'

Then she walked into the shop and looked at the jewellery idly. The shop was quite crowded. She was sure no one else could have known that Kalishankar had given her jewellery. But someone definitely did. Someone out there knew a lot more than she could have imagined. The boy was standing guard outside the shop. Chintamoni had worried and fretted so much that, at some point, she'd finally reached the end of her tether. Since then, she'd reached some kind of understanding with the divine. Whatever had to happen would happen. She couldn't lose her courage now.

Before the police searched the kitchen, she had considered, even if only for a moment, throwing herself at their feet and admitting her crime—at least half her guilt—hadn't she?

The shopkeeper asked, 'Tell me, Bou-di, what would you like to see?'

She said, 'My granddaughter is a year-and-a-half old, so I was thinking of buying her a pearl necklace with a locket. Fake pearls, of course. Do you have gold lockets, nothing too heavy?'

'Of course we do. Just the kind you want. I can show you lockets with high prices or low, whichever you prefer. Here, look at these.'

'Show me, please. But I'll only take a look today. I'll buy it next month.'

'You can place an order if you want to, and then come next month and...'

When Chintamoni left Bowbazar, she decided to take no risks and hailed a taxi. 'Kalighat Temple,' she said.

Her trip had been futile. She'd only ended up wasting a lot of money on the taxi fare. No matter how much she puzzled over it, Chintamoni just couldn't work out what was happening.

Was the inquisitive boy in Bowbazar somehow linked to the hidden treasure? No, how could that be? Nearly two years had passed since Kalishankar's death. This was the first time she'd stepped outside all by herself. Besides visiting the grocery shop near the temple, she hardly ever left the house. If she thought about it logically, it was possible that someone had been keeping an eye on them for several years, but...

This question became the new source of Chintamoni's worries. A few days later, Balai Haldar came downstairs and told Manmatha, 'Look, Manmatha, Kalishankar's death keeps bringing new troubles into our life. Lots of people think we have gold and jewellery hidden somewhere. You get what I mean? They think we've grabbed a large part of the stolen jewellery. And then you know what the maids are like. Sanaka always exaggerates everything. Who knows what stories she's been telling? People believe her too. I've told her so many times not to lie so much. She just doesn't listen. Sanaka can't keep her mouth shut. My beyaan told me the other day, "You can say what you like but I'm sure you haven't handed everything over to the police." What do I say to this? I got so angry. But they're my daughter's in-laws, I can't just swear at them. So I had to stomach it!'

Manmatha told Balai Haldar, 'Sit down, Haldar Moshai, sit down and tell me everything.'

Balai Haldar shook his head. 'I haven't told you yet—yesterday I saw someone had dug up the ground near the neem tree. Who was it? When did they do it? The keys have been with me the whole time. I got so worried. What if it was an attempted robbery?'

'Of course not, why should it be a robbery? No matter what happens elsewhere in the neighbourhood, I'm sure thieves won't come here,' Manmatha said, smiling reassuringly.

'Anyway, my brother and I have agreed to keep the front door locked from 11 in the morning. It's quite clear criminals are on our trail. Tell the women—the front door will remain locked from now on.'

Sumantra was lying in bed reading *Arabian Nights*. Now he said, 'One day on my way back from school a couple of boys called out to me near Abinash's house and said, "Listen, you have a lot of gold hidden in your house, don't you?" I said, "No, everything has been handed over to the police." Then he pulled my cheek and said, "How well you've learnt to lie, my sweet boy. Why are you so skinny? Doesn't your father feed you? He has a lot of money. Tell him to give you two glasses of milk and two eggs every day, all right?" Then they started cackling at me.'

Chintamoni stood looking at her son, frozen in fear. Sharbari stood close to her mother and said, 'So frightening, Ma!'

Lying in bed at night, Chintamoni regretted everything that had taken place. Perhaps it was Kalishankar's infatuation with her that had made him stay for so long. She'd always protested when he wanted to leave. Maybe if he hadn't been entangled with her, he'd have left and wouldn't have been murdered. And all this fear and apprehension wouldn't have darkened Chintamoni's life.

Manmatha had been sleeping in the other room for quite some time. Chintamoni slept in the larger room with their children. Unable to bear it anymore, Chintamoni got up and went to her husband. Manmatha was always eager to have sex with her, but Chintamoni never gave him a chance. When she called out to him tonight, he immediately pulled his wife down onto the bed. Chintamoni let go of herself for some time. When Manmatha entered her, she wrapped both legs around his waist. Manmatha said, 'Chinu, you're not the old Chinu anymore. You've changed so much. You never wrapped your legs around me before.'

Chintamoni replied, 'Uff, don't talk so much! Just do what you're doing properly. Are you even a man?'

Once they'd finished, she said, 'Let's leave this house and go somewhere else. I don't like this place anymore. Everything's going wrong. This one incident has been clinging to our life like a shadow!'

'What do you mean?' said Manmatha. 'These are small things. Just people nosing around. How can we leave this house? Do you think we'll find a house at this rent in a decent neighbourhood? The owners don't even bother about the rent these days. It's the perfect place to stay all our lives. Why should we leave it?'

Chintamoni said, 'Will we never have our own house then? A one-storey house? A roof over our heads?'

'Hah! So that's what you dream about.' Manmatha grew sad. 'We have no hope. If Sumantra gets better and is well-established, maybe then.'

Chintamoni put her hand on Manmatha's back and said, 'There's something I always think about telling you. But I'm not sure what you'll say, so I've never told you. You're already weighed down with responsibilities. You might start crying like a child if I tell you, and then everyone will come to know. I can't trust you at all.'

Manmatha said, 'Tell me, tell me, my lips are sealed.'

'It isn't enough to seal your mouth, you must tie your hands and feet too.'

'Should I then?' he asked.

Manmatha sat quietly, rocking back and forth.

'Will you listen?' she snapped. 'I have gold. Do you understand?'

Manmatha buried his face in his knees.

'Why don't you speak?'

'I understand.' Manmatha sighed heavily. 'Where did you find it?'

'I'd gone to Himani's house to attend her wedding. I saw a bundle of red cloth hanging from the top of the room on our roof, on the side of the small terrace. I knew what it was right away.'

'Hanging?'

'I mean, it was fixed to the ring at the mouth of the horizontal pipe for draining rainwater.'

'Really?'

'I've hidden it under the coal heap in the kitchen.'

Manmatha said, 'Chinu, what would have happened if we got caught during the search?'

'The investigation was over by then. Himani got married only two months ago.'

'Chinu, you're lying. All those boys live in the room on the roof and not one of them saw it all this time?'

'I was fated to get it!'

Manmatha started shaking his head. 'No, no, no. This is not right! This is a sin! It's a sin! Don't take this gold, don't keep it.'

'All right, then you go tell the police. I'll return it.'

Manmatha began hitting his forehead with his palm. 'They'll put us all in jail, all of us.'

'Then what should we do?'

'Let's go and throw it all in the Ganga, Chinu.'

'What will I do with this gold if you don't want to keep it? I can't just go and sell it, can I?'

'No, don't you dare! Don't you dare!'

'So we must throw it away?'

'Why did you tell me, Chinu? Why? You've snatched the little sleep I get at night.'

'Oh, and you're a saint, aren't you?'

'Me?'

'You plan to spend all your life in someone else's house. You call that honourable?'

'I have no other option. But I do pay the rent!'

Chintamoni returned as quietly to her room as she'd left it and lay down. So he wanted to get rid of it? She'd like to see him try. What a fool.

About a week later Manmatha said, 'How much gold is it, Chinu?'

'Enough to get Sharbari married and buy a house. We can even afford an operation for Sumantra,' she said with a smile, wiping her sweat.

That night, Manmatha suddenly held her hand and started sobbing. 'If I die, you'll have nothing else to worry about, Chinu.'

'Wonderful, go celebrate. You never even bought me a gold nose ring all these years.'

# 5

Chintamoni said, 'Never mind Puri or Darjeeling or Kashmir, you never even took me to Chandannagar. The Jagaddhatri Pujo lights, Siraj's Tomb—there was so much I wanted to see. You never took me to the cinema or to the theatre. Just to the zoo and the museum. We don't even visit anyone. I'm afraid to spend too much money, so I don't go to weddings to avoid buying gifts. I've spent my whole life repressing all my wishes and desires. I can't even visit my granddaughter often because I'll have to take her a gift. Let me take care of my own needs by myself now. Who's stopping you from dying?'

Glaring at her husband, Chintamoni left the room. Three days passed. Manmatha wasn't home yet. Evening turned into late night. Sharbari and Sumantra went to someone's house some distance from theirs and phoned the businessmen's office in Burrabazar where Manmatha worked, but no one answered. Balai Haldar and Sadhan Haldar started looking for him, but without success. Around 1 a.m. the police arrived along with three or four of their neighbours. Balai Haldar came downstairs quickly. The police asked, 'Which of you is Manmathababu's relative?'

Balai Haldar asked one of their neighbours, 'What's happened, Satyabrata?'

'Balaida, come outside for a second.'

Chintamoni couldn't even bring herself to weep. Who knew what Manmatha had done? Maybe he'd gone to the police himself. For a bewildered moment she thought suicide was all fate had in store for her now.

Outside, Satyabrata told Balai Haldar, 'You know Aparesh is one of the medical staff at the hospital.'

'Yes, I do.'

'Today, a man took a taxi from Dharmatala and asked to be driven around the Maidan for an hour. Suddenly the driver realised the passenger wasn't speaking anymore. He'd slid down in his seat. When the driver couldn't get a response from him, he took him to Medical College. The doctors declared the man dead. The police went, and Aparesh saw the crowd and looked in and found it was Manmatha.'

Just as the sky had been about to come crashing down on their heads, Chintamoni found it had stopped midway. Since Manmatha had been their employee for a long time, the Suranas didn't neglect to pay the rest of his salary to his cursed, helpless family.

Urmila said, 'Ma, I'll send money for the rent now and then. Don't worry.' But all this help was hardly of any use to Chintamoni. Given the amount of gold she had, she reflected, there was no cause for worry. She did have to give up her marriage bangles and sindoor and stop eating fish, but at least she wouldn't end up begging on the streets. She'd find some way to sell the gold, even if in small amounts. But Sharbari didn't want to study anymore. Both children had fallen into despair. Sumantra, after all, was still a boy—he'd keep asking the same question all day, 'Ma, what will happen to us now? What will happen?'

There were no answers Chintamoni could give to console him. A few months later, Sharbari said, 'Ma, I've found a job, a good one. I can't sit around. I'm no good at studies anyway, and I can't get married right now. Who will look after you if I marry? I've decided what I want to do.'

She was 18 or 19, an attractive girl. She dressed in saris now and had a slender figure and cascading hair. Her face resembled her mother's but was darker. Sharbari had no time to plait her locks, and neither did she want to. She just tied them up in a bun. When she did, she suddenly looked very grown up.

A new shop had come up on Rashbehari Avenue; it sold made-to-order blouses and dresses for women. Lovely's Own. A woman named Lovely Singh was the owner. The shop occupied both floors of a two-storey building. The first floor was used to stock fabric and to take measurements and orders. The measurements for women were taken behind a curtain. The ground floor was the delivery counter. Lovely Singh's shop had a speciality—just like the owner, all the employees were women. However, the tailors working in the factory behind the building were all men. They cut and stitched blouses and made the clothes, but all the work inside the shop was done by women. They took measurements and orders and cut fabric in colours matching the saris. They delivered the clothes, managed the cash, and even cleaned the shop and served tea and snacks. These women were a little different from most others. Lovely Singh used Lovely's Own for social service of a sort. Most of the women working in the shop came from poor families. Or they were people cheated by fate, or young, helpless widows, or spinsters rejected for their lack of wealth and beauty, or orphans. These were the kinds of women she employed. Lovely Singh worked on the first floor. They managed the shop together like a joint family.

What Sharbari had got wasn't exactly a proper job. There was a new trend of sewing a border on the edge of a sari to make it fall gracefully to the ground. This border was called the 'fall'. In the past, since women usually stayed at home, they wore simple saris. But now they went out quite often—to schools, colleges, offices. So they dressed up in all sorts of ways. They often wore georgette or silk saris and attached falls to them. The fall made it easy to arrange the pleats of the sari and also prevented it from getting soiled. This way, the actual border didn't fray easily. Attaching a fall had become so normal that those who didn't do it were considered inept at urban life. Lovely's Own also accepted orders for attaching falls to saris and had begun getting them in large numbers. South Kolkata's fashionable women needed separate blouses and falls for every sari, and even picot stitches for the ends of these saris.

Sharbari took up the work of attaching falls and doing picot stitches. She was quite skilled at sewing. Besides, she lived close by and had been a resident of the area for a long time. Seeing her abject poverty, Shipra had told Lovely Singh about Sharbari and arranged a means of income for her. She collected the saris, attached the falls, and did the picot stitches at home in two or three days and returned them to the shop. Each sari brought her one rupee, and the shop supplied her with the falls. You couldn't just entrust a stranger with customers' expensive saris, so the precautions were necessary.

On the first day, Sharbari returned home with five saris, accompanied by Shipra and Shyamali. Sharbari left her mother to chat with them and quickly made tea. Shipra said, 'Now, Sharbari, don't end up embarrassing me, all right? Lay a mat out on your bed when you sew, and don't drink tea or anything when you're working. Don't work when your hands are wet or oily. Don't do things like eating muri with onion when working. And no matter how much you're tempted, don't you dare put on the customers' saris. The shop shouldn't be disgraced. The girls are working hard to manage it with dignity.'

Sharbari said, 'Don't worry, Shipra. No harm will come to the saris while I'm here.'

'You haven't heard of incidents like these, have you? Go on Shyamali, tell her! There have even been cases of dressing in a customer's sari during the visit of a prospective groom's family.'

Chintamoni sat there listening to their conversation. Suddenly she asked, 'How long will it take you to complete work on five saris?'

'I'll complete it in one day, Ma!' Sharbari said with enthusiasm.

Shyamali said, 'This energy will last for only two days. After that you'll find you can't even straighten your shoulders. Do it slowly, that's how you'll complete it in time. Where's the sense in working for two days and then lying in bed for the next two?'

Shyamali and Shipra laughed. Before they left, they said, 'Put the saris in a cupboard. Don't forget they aren't yours!'

When they went outside, Shyamali said to Shipra, 'Sharbari's mother seems a bit off in the head, doesn't she? Her eyes are so blank. But she's so beautiful. God, you can't take your eyes off her.'

Shipra said, 'She wasn't like this before, this is how she is now, dull and quiet.'

'Poor family. Now this young girl will have to earn a living for them. Do you think she'll manage?'

'Why not? I've done it, you've done it too. I was 23 when my husband died. Who do you think looked after my widowed mother-in-law and unmarried sister-in-law?'

After stitching falls on saris for five days, Sharbari took to her bed. Then she got out of it and started working again. Chintamoni told her, 'I need to go out for something. I'm leaving now. You keep working. There's rice in the pot, don't forget to eat.'

Sharbari said, 'Ma, don't you dare. Stop this madness now. You're not going anywhere. You're barely sane anymore. Do you want to get run over by a car? Be quiet and sit here.'

Chintamoni just couldn't explain how important it was for her to go out. She had to. She couldn't bear to see her daughter having to work so hard. In her head she said, *You idiot! We're not poor, we're not poor. I'll get you married, I'll look after Sumantra, I'll do everything. Don't wear yourself out this way*. But she never had the courage to tell her daughter the truth. The price of gold shot up suddenly, going past 300 rupees. Chintamoni decided to wait a little longer.

Two more years went by as she waited. By then Sharbari had taken over the task of earning for the family.

She now made 150 rupees a month—enough to ensure two meals a day for the three of them. Urmila paid the rent, and sometimes they received the interest from their savings. Sharbari woke up early in the morning to light the stove in the kitchen and start working. She took off her nightclothes, made tea, and bought milk and groceries. A little later she opened her umbrella and left for Lovely's Own with a heavy black bag. She deposited the saris she had finished working on and returned with new orders within an hour. Chintamoni couldn't do anything these days, besides a bit of cooking. Chintamoni kept asking herself, why couldn't she? Why couldn't she? What was the problem? But her hands and feet refused to move. Once the dal and rice were made, Sumantra ate and left for school. When Sharbari returned, she took a bath and turned on the radio. As she listened, she rapidly stitched falls on the saris. After eating and resting in the afternoon, she began working again. Sometimes she'd cry out, 'Ouch, my finger!' In the evening it was Sharbari again who lit the stove and made rotis and vegetables for them. The siblings had started living in the bigger room. Chintamoni spent the day on the bed in the small room. She turned off the lights and spoke very little. Nipobithi would call out to her from the lane outside sometimes. 'What have you been up to, Chinu? Come here, talk to me. You'll stop talking altogether if you go on this way.'

Chintamoni couldn't even think of leaving the house anymore. Besides one or two pieces of jewellery, everything she had got had been lying beneath the coal heap for years and years. Chintamoni bought coal as soon as it began to run out. If Sharbari said, 'There's enough, we can buy it later,' Chintamoni grew furious with her. She'd be very pleased when coal was delivered from the nearby coal depot. The delivery man would write '7/Bha/1/3/-' on the wall with coal. It was a receipt that meant: 7th of the month of Bhadra, one sack of coal, three rupees.

Standing by the window covered with netting, Chintamoni would chat briefly with Nipobithi and then go back to bed.

Sumantra had matured greatly in the past few years. He was 12 or 13 now, slim and tall with a perpetual smile on his dark face. He was very good at his studies. He didn't need tutoring in subjects besides maths, and he scored very well in all of them.

Sharbari was proud of her brother. She'd say, 'Bhai, you can be anything you want to be, a doctor or an engineer. I'll pay for your studies.'

But Sumantra would say, 'Didi, I want to be a chartered accountant. I love counting and doing sums.'

Sharbari would reply, 'Whatever you want, I'll pay for it. If you study to become a CA you'll get a good job. They'll send cars to pick you up and drop you off after work. You'll wear a tie when you go to your office. You'll buy a flat in a rich neighbourhood and get a doorbell. When you press it, a bird will call coo-coo-coo-coo. You must get a big dog then, all right? As soon as the doorbell goes coo-coo, the dog will start barking and drive your neighbours crazy. Then your wife will scold the dog in English.'

Chintamoni would sit up in bed and nod wildly when she heard these exchanges. It was all possible. Oh, her children didn't even know the truth.

Sumantra had been quite healthy of late and wasn't falling ill as often as he used to. If Chintamoni had still been sane, he alone would have given her enough motivation to live. After all, children were one of the main reasons a family ran smoothly. If she hadn't lost her mind, Chintamoni would have realised that every mother and father wished for a son like Sumantra. If she'd still been in her senses, her face would always have glowed with pride at having given birth to a daughter like Sharbari. Such talent, sacrifice, and hard work! The girl had so much patience and virtue. But Chintamoni had long drifted away from the world around her. Secrets and the hidden treasure—that's all her life was. It was as though Chintamoni was sitting before a plate heaped with chicken and fish bones and chewing on them. There was nothing else on the plate—no rice, no dal, no vegetables. She could chew on the bones but never bring herself to actually eat them.

One day Sumantra returned from school and went to watch a football match nearby. The poor boy couldn't play himself, he just enjoyed watching the game. When the ball came his way, he was glad to get a chance to pass it back. Sumantra's friend from Haldarpara, Manish, was a decent player. If Sumantra managed to kick the ball back once or twice, his lips would curve upwards in a smile. Manish played while Sumantra watched. The game was getting heated. People crowded around, booing and cheering, clapping and whistling, when suddenly the ball came flying towards Sumantra. Before he knew it a strong blow to the chest knocked him down on the ground. Manish and the others rushed to him.

'Are you all right? Did you get hurt?' Manish asked.

Sumantra scrunched up his face and said, 'Yes, it hurts quite a lot.' He sat up and smiled meekly.

Manish said, 'Come on, let's go home.'

Sumantra began to ask, 'Aren't you going on with the game?' Instead, a stream of blood trickled out of his mouth. Taken aback, he tried to say, 'Take me home,' when another stream came out. Sumantra wanted to say, 'Didi? Ma?' but blood flooded his chest.

Sumantra died that very night in the emergency ward of PG Hospital.

# 6

Women who work hard to make a living begin to show signs of their labour on their bodies. Sharbari's body too had begun to reveal her exhaustion in the last couple of years. She was barely 23, but she resembled a middle-aged spinster. Many young women these days marry only after their Bachelor's and Master's degrees are completed, nothing unusual about that. But when you saw Sharbari you couldn't help thinking, 'Poor thing. She never got married and now the constant exertion is ruining her looks.'

A permanent expression of annoyance had set in on Sharbari's face. She'd lost her usually patient demeanour. Even trivial things infuriated her. Any grace she once had was gone. She went about her bath and meals perfunctorily and wore her sari untidily. She tied her hair into a bun without untangling it. The bindi of kajal she wore on her forehead made her look even less attractive. Around this time, Gopal, the matchmaker from their neighbourhood, came round with a marriage prospect for Sharbari. The boy was 'good', since he was very well-educated, but the family's financial situation was precarious. In fact, it was inexplicably perilous. He had eight dark-skinned, plain-looking sisters and lived in a rented house with a tin roof. The sisters were unmarried and the father had tuberculosis. Despite this, instead of getting a job he had started a chemicals factory near Park Circus after borrowing a lot of money. He'd been looking to get married to pay off some of the loans. Gopal knew very well that no one would willingly let their daughter marry him. But then no one could predict what girls' fathers would do. If their daughter grew old, they often acted in desperation. There was no other reason for anyone to mortgage their homes to get their daughters married.

For a long time, Gopal had assumed that the landowners and tenants of Kalachand Haldar's house had grabbed what they could after the murder and had kept their mouths shut. But after witnessing Chintamoni's unending misfortunes, Gopal was sure that they didn't have any hidden treasure. The mother was mad, the son was dead, and the daughter had withered from working long hours. Certainly no one had luck as bad as theirs! If this man married Sharbari, then she would at least get rid of the label of spinsterhood. The man could live here and manage his factory, and Sharbari's income could help run the household. That too was a kind of dowry, after all.

The prospective groom accompanied Gopal to inspect Sharbari. She made tea for Indubrata and started chatting casually with him. As he watched Sharbari sew falls onto saris, Indubrata added a few stitches himself.

Sharbari said, 'You're quite good at this!'

'Of course! I know all kinds of work.'

'But you're the first son after eight sisters. You must have been a spoiled brat.'

Indubrata smiled. 'I never lived at home. I used to live in a friend's house to study in peace. They had piles of books. I think I read every book they had!'

'Oh!' Sharbari said. 'Would you like an omelette?'

'Yes.'

'Wait then, I'll make you one.'

'I'll come with you. Let's see how good your omelette is,' Indubrata said, looking at Sharbari as though he was asking for permission. Meanwhile, Chintamoni was lost in her thoughts. When she'd heard the words 'chemicals factory', something had come to life in her head. What was it now, what was it? It was on the tip of her tongue. Oh, it was so suffocating here, she could never remember things. In her efforts to recall, she crossed and uncrossed her eyebrows as though she was exercising them. Indubrata too was a slightly eccentric man. He had all kinds of strange, compulsive habits. Every now and then he'd stretch his back and shoulders and crack his knuckles loudly. Sometimes he'd shake his hands so vigorously that it would irritate anyone nearby. When Indubrata saw Chintamoni furrowing her brow over and over again, he started laughing loudly. Gopal the matchmaker thought, *This has worked out well. This man is a nutcase too. They'll figure out how to put up with one another.* He said, 'Indubrata, since you'll be here for some time, I'll just go and collect another girl's photograph from her house nearby. The girl is quite thin, so I asked her father to get new photos. They need to seat her in a small chair for the photos. Have you seen the chairs children sit in? Something like that. Only then will she look a bit healthy. Let me go and see how the pictures turned out. I'll bc back soon.'

As soon as Gopal left, a smile lit up Chintamoni's face. She said, 'So you have a chemicals factory?'

Indubrata said, 'Yes.'

Chintamoni lost track of the conversation. She sank into her own thoughts again. Suddenly she remembered: coal! Yes, coal! She asked Indubrata, 'Can you melt coal in your factory?'

Indubrata said, 'No, Mashima, we don't melt coal there. But I did meet someone in Allahabad who was trying to make cola shondesh. A Bengali scientist.'

'Oh, then he's of no use,' said Chintamoni. With all her memories of the hidden gold gone, coal was slowly consuming Chintamoni's mind. Long ago, in her childhood, she'd heard her youngest uncle tell a story about Dibrugarh or someplace, where he'd gone into a coal mine. The tunnel was very rugged and uneven. There was complete darkness, a clanging noise inside the mine, the sound of a lift descending into its depths. The sound of pickaxes and shovels and crumbling rock, and the miners' sighs of despair at the searchlight going out. Darkness and more darkness, and coal—huge, rough blocks of coal. Those were the images that came back to her. Sharbari took Indubrata into the kitchen.

Topenbabu's wife and a few others peeped in now and then. Times had changed greatly. Conservative thought was being challenged every day, in every field of life. So what if Sharbari did end up getting married? Indubrata sat on a stool after rolling up his trousers. Sharbari fetched the kitchen blade to slice onions and chillies. She'd never especially wanted to get married, so she was quite calm. She asked, 'Do you eat spicy food?'

'I eat a lot of spicy food. I'm a Bangal after all!'

'Then I'll add a lot of chillies?'

'Go ahead!'

'Will you have a double egg omelette?'

'Of course, that would be fantastic,' Indubrata said, laughing. 'I can smell something in your kitchen!'

'A bad smell?' asked Sharbari, slightly embarrassed.

'There are no bad or good smells for me. All smells are just different chemical compositions.'

'What do you smell, tell me.'

'I smell gold.'

Sharbari stared at him. The man was completely mad. She asked, 'Does gold have a smell?'

'It does. But it's hard to smell the essential elements. You need a specialised nose.'

Sharbari started laughing. 'My god, what a nose.'

'My nose is extraordinary,' said Indubrata.

'It's not just you, everyone in our house smells gold here.' She lowered her voice. 'Did you know, there is supposedly a lot of gold hidden in our house. Hidden treasure.'

Indubrata nodded wisely. 'They're right, there is. It's hidden somewhere right here. I can smell it very clearly!'

Eating his omelette with great relish, Indubrata left. Sharbari slapped her forehead. 'I can barely put up with one nutcase, and now another one's come along!' She forgot about the incident. Every day she stitched falls on three or four saris. Now she earned almost two and a half rupees for each sari. Ten more years passed this way. No more marriage prospects came Sharbari's way. It was hard to get a girl married when everyone knew her mother was mad.

The four owners of the Haldar house decided to sell it. There was just one problem—two of its tenants had lived there for nearly 50 years. After much begging, Topenbabu agreed to leave with a payment of 20,000 rupees. Satyaki and Kakoli moved elsewhere of their own free will. Sharbari was also paid 30,000 rupees and given a year's time to leave the house. Now they would have only two rooms, since the rooms on the other side of the courtyard would slowly be broken down and rebuilt. The two rooms on the opposite side were where Sharbari's family would have to live. They'd cook in one room and sleep in another. Soon enough, it would be time for them to leave.

Sharbari immediately started looking for rooms to rent. No matter what, she had to live in Kalighat, or Lovely's Own wouldn't give her work. If Lovely Singh was strict about rules, her daughter Amrita was 10 times worse. Amrita was about 30 and looked after the shop now.

One day the Haldars packed up their belongings and left the house. Locks hung on every door. Besides the two of them, there wasn't a single soul left in the house. All day the house remained quiet—sometimes pigeons could be heard cooing. The lifeless building began to appear even more derelict and ugly.

They'd have to clear out of the kitchen early the next morning. Annoyed, Sharbari set aside her usual work and began to empty out the kitchen. She threw out a lot of useless things. She kept boxes, containers, and utensils in the smaller room. A sense of indifference drove her to break the kiln with a hammer. But it wouldn't break easily now. The kiln had been tended to for so many decades. Her grandmother had cooked in it, her mother had cooked in it, and even she had used it. But now Sharbari used the Janata stove for everything.

Once everything had been cleared out, Chintamoni got to her feet and came to take a look. 'The coal?' she asked.

Sharbari snapped at her. 'What will you use the coal for, my funeral?'

'But we need it.'

'No, we don't. Now go on, go take your bath.'

Chintamoni said, 'Oh.' Then she went and lay down again. She wondered and wondered. There was some way she was connected to that heap of coal. A strange glow poured out of it. It enchanted her. It hypnotised her. Teased by the faintest memories, Chintamoni slowly fell asleep from exhaustion.

The next morning, the new landlord's men arrived with mechanics and labourers. After checking the house, they fixed a new lock on the kitchen door.

# The Household

# 1

Four days had passed since the end of the mourning period, but there were still so many people in the house. Tota had been staying there with her two children since the day after Baba's death. But then she was Anamitra's father-in-law's daughter, so it was natural that she would stay. Anamitra had no objections there. But why should Mou keep living in the house with her husband and son? Because when Mou had lost her own father as a child, her uncle had looked after her like his own child. For Mou, losing Parimal Mukherjee was like losing her father. So Mou had fasted and performed the daughter's part of the funeral rites as well as the rites meant to end the mourning period. But then she hadn't budged from the house for the next two weeks. What if Mou decided to stay as long as Tota did? Yesterday, Anamitra had heard Tota and Mou discussing that, until it was time for their children to go to school, they could easily live here in their paternal home.

Neither Tota nor Mou's children had been enrolled in school yet.

Anamitra's daughter Sohini went to a boarding school. She had come home for three days after her grandfather's death and then left again. Anamitra had deliberately sent her daughter to boarding school—she hadn't wanted Sohini to grow up in this congested, noisy house. Something or the other was always being celebrated, besides endless visits from relatives. Anyone who dropped in simply pulled out one of the chairs lined up at their huge dining table and sat down to eat. And her mother-in-law chewed paan and sweetly called out, 'Make sure to feed them before they leave, Bou-ma!'

Anamitra prickled with anger. She was always irritated these days. And why shouldn't she be? True, there was a family business, a huge and profitable one—in fact, it was like Goddess Lakshmi herself lived in their house—and she never seemed to leave. But her father-in-law had stopped managing the business a long time ago. It was Siddhartha who had been slaving away to provide money for the family all these years. And his health was getting worse every day. He'd developed high blood pressure as early as his forties. Siddhartha never ate the elaborate spread that was cooked in the house every day. He worked too much and ate too little, he didn't even have time for yoga classes in the morning. So why shouldn't Anamitra want him to stop carrying the weight of the family and look after himself? To work a little less than he did now and relax at the end of the day? As for herself, some day she would pass out from the amount of work she had to do. This constant need to entertain guests—Anamitra couldn't take it anymore.

While her father-in-law was alive, he had never complained, and matters had remained as they were. But he had told Siddhartha, 'You can let things go on this way if you want, but I want a break. I will go live in the Golf Green flat, and you can handle this chaos on your own.'

Siddhartha had agreed with him. 'Yes, we need to stop this extravagance. The business isn't doing well either. You have to explain to Ma that we cannot keep spending so much on guests.'

'The real problem is this house. Everyone knows that there's no dearth of space here. There are so many empty rooms. You should get a smaller house, a three-room flat. This house is so big and so old. We don't need all this space. What's the use of maintaining such a large establishment? We spend 500 rupees a month on insect repellent. Your mother just asks us to ring pest control and thinks her job is done.'

Besides Tota and Mou, there was also Anamitra's mother-in-law's younger sister and her slightly peculiar, unmarried older daughter, Anamika. And of all places, Anamika had occupied the room right next to Anamitra's. A long time ago, when Anamitra had just got married, she had given Anamika special care so as to come across as a good, warm-hearted person. She lent a new sari to Anamika and even gave away a perfume she'd received as a wedding present. She told her, 'Our names are so similar, Chhoto-mashi, I'm sure we'll be good friends.'

But the nutjob had clung to Anamitra like a leech ever since, following her around all day and driving her crazy with her whining. Well, served Anamitra right for indulging her. The other day, Anamika had taken the petticoat Anamitra had hung out to dry on the terrace and had left bloodstains on it! Anamitra had nearly exploded with anger. She could have slapped her then. Aww, what an innocent little girl, feeding rice to crows on the balcony—but who would clean up the mess she left behind every day?

The other residents of the house included her father-in-law's sister's husband, who had lost his wife. There was also Sanatan—whom Anamitra's mother-in-law treated as a son—and his wife. Ma had once fallen sick during a visit to the Tarapith temple. She had had to stay at Sanatan's house there—he and his wife had looked after her with great care. They too had settled here the day after Baba's death and showed no signs of leaving.

Two of Tota's friends from college, Ruchira and Sarbani, came by in the evening. Tota chatted away with them in her room on the third floor. Mou was with them as well. Soon, Tota called out, 'Will you send us some tea, Bou-di?'

It hardly seemed as if her father had just died. In fact, the girls seemed to have come to have a good time. But Anamitra had other worries when it came to Tota. She wasn't going to inherit the business—its ownership had been transferred to Siddhartha a long time ago. But what about her father-in-law's own money and gold? All of it would go to Tota.

Anamitra realised her father-in-law had been a unique sort of man. Extremely refined, a big spender, and very generous. He had a hobby—he collected antique tea sets, crockery, and cutlery. Over the years, Parimal Mukherjee had collected nearly 40 tea sets. Some of them were made in Victorian times. One of them had a picture of Queen Elizabeth's wedding embossed on it—what a beautiful set it was.

But the most expensive and beautiful of them all was the deep blue one. It was patterned with blood-red roses and had gold plating. Tota wanted to divide up the inheritance, and she wanted the deep blue dinner set and tea set for herself. But Anamitra would never let that happen. She would acquire that tea set at any cost. She was no longer the shy young girl she'd been just after her marriage. She had to be tough about these things, because Siddhartha never would be.

That was all she'd been thinking about the past few days. She'd been calculating and rationalising, preparing arguments, just in case the matter of the inheritance was brought up. She'd had enough of living under her mother-in-law's thumb. Asha had been presiding over the household for too many years, she was too deeply invested in its affairs. It wasn't like she'd be able to take this household with her to the afterlife. She should have handed over the responsibility to Anamitra by now. But no, she would never let go of it so easily. Someone who worried over family matters as she wept on the way to her husband's cremation would not relinquish the reins of the household anytime soon. When Baba was being lifted into the glass funeral carriage, Anamitra's mother Ashima had begun to giggle at what Asha was saying.

When Anamitra asked her later, 'Why were you laughing?', her mother said, 'How could I not? Her own husband was about to burn on the pyre, but did you hear what your mother-in-law was talking about? "Sidhu, make sure everyone who goes for the cremation comes back to the house, no one should be left out." Who would think of such things at that time? Shame on her! I have a household to manage too, but I'm not worrying about guests when I'm supposed to be numb from grief.'

Anamitra told her mother, 'You should have heard what she was saying earlier. Baba had been laid out in his own room, and everyone who arrived was going there directly. So she took me aside and said, "Listen Bou-ma, there are lots of expensive things in your baba's room. Something might just get stolen. Ask Sidhu to arrange for him to be laid out in the veranda, okay?" I mean, he's not an object!'

'Oh god. She seems so sweet, like she enjoys inviting people home and feeding them, but now I see she's quite sly.'

Anamitra laughed. 'She changes colours all the time, didn't you know?'

For a few years, Anamitra had remained indifferent to household matters simply because she had to put up with her mother-in-law's deep obsession with them. Her daughter was away at boarding school, so she tried to escape to her parental home whenever she got the opportunity. Anamitra's mother was a strange woman and was slightly disorganised in her ways. She could chat away for hours after having lunch without washing her hands. She often burnt the milk by accident and wailed when it boiled over. She had observed that everything in the household was run by Anamitra's mother-in-law, while Anamitra had more of an executive role. Asha took all the decisions, Anamitra had to perform her bidding. She was tired of playing this role. When her father-in-law transferred the business to Siddhartha, Anamitra began thinking about her own rights. She began to wonder when she would be given some authority too. Anamitra's sister Malabika managed her household herself after her mother-in-law had transferred its responsibility to her. Malabika could do whatever she wanted, Malabika was free. Anamitra wanted to be free like her. And after her father-in-law's death, she had begun to feel brave.

Anamitra had been preparing herself. When Jyotirmay Uncle came over in the evening, Anamitra noticed her mother-in-law taking him into Baba's room. Her suspicions arose when she saw Asha close the door. She quickly rang Siddhartha. 'Listen, Ma is discussing something with Jyotirmay Kaka and she has closed the door of the room.'

Siddhartha said, 'I know, I know. Baba has left the details of his will with Jyotirmay Kaka. That's probably what Ma wants to know about. But why are you worried? The business and the house belong to me. Tota doesn't have a share in either.'

'I heard Baba has left something for Mou too. That's why she's been staying in the house so long.'

'Look, Baba has done what he wanted. I shouldn't interfere.'

'But you shouldn't ignore it either.'

When she hung up and went outside her room, she found her mother-in-law looking for her. 'Jyoti is here, Bou-ma. Bring him some tea and snacks. And have you fed Tota's friends upstairs? Did you give them tea? They arrived a while ago.'

Anamitra had been waiting for an opportunity like this. She said, 'Ma, what do you think of me? You think I don't know we must serve tea to guests? I've spent so many years in this house. You behave like I came here yesterday, like I don't understand anything. As if the household will fall apart if you don't tell me what to do.'

Her mother-in-law stared at her, bewildered. 'No, why are you getting angry, Bou-ma? I've never ordered you around.'

'So what? Ma, I worked hard to get an MA, and nothing that I studied is useful to me now. I've come to understand the household well enough after the training you gave me. I no longer like being told what to do all the time. You should hand over all of this to me now. I'll manage it better than you do. If you have complaints, you can tell me.'

Her mother-in-law said, 'What should I leave to you?'

There was something in her tone that unsettled Anamitra a bit. She said, 'What do you suppose? I will handle the household from now on. You don't need to bother about it anymore. You can spend your time with your gods and your rituals.'

Her mother-in-law grew more bewildered. 'But, Bou-ma, I am a housewife. All the rituals are for the welfare of my children! I've never asked god for anything for myself. All I've wanted is your well-being—'

Anamitra interrupted her. 'I don't see how that's helping us. I know a large family often has guests, but we can't have people crowding the house all year round. If only you'd try to understand your son's difficulties, Ma.

Prices are shooting up, but we waste so much money on needless expenditures. I'm not the only one who thinks so. Your son has told me this himself. You're just content to bark orders because, after all, you don't have to worry about money.'

At this moment, Jyoti Kaka emerged from the room and said, 'Anamitra isn't wrong. Siddhartha was telling me the same thing that day. Bou-di, you should let her take over the household now. Your term has come to an end. Now it's their household to manage, let them do as they see fit.'

Anamitra said, 'Think about it, Jyoti Kaka. I mean, Baba has just passed away, but Ma is behaving like there's a celebration in the house. She's always boasting about having a full family, but we're the ones who suffer trying to keep it that way. And the ones Ma wastes so much effort on are the ones who nitpick the most.'

Ma said, 'Is that true?'

Tota was coming downstairs with her friends; the sound of their laughter could be heard. Anamitra said, 'Jyoti Kaka, am I wrong? Look, my cousin is getting married tomorrow. The mourning period has long been over, I could easily go to the wedding if I wanted to. But I am still so miserable about Baba. I've lived here so long, and I've always considered him my father. But I don't understand how Tota, his own daughter, can manage to gossip away with her friends. And Ma? Bring this, do that, this rule, that rule—that's all she's done since Baba's death. I haven't seen her mourn him one bit.'

Her mother-in-law collapsed into a chair. She began to sob. 'You're saying whatever you want to, Bou-ma!'

Anamitra exhaled forcefully and said, 'Yes, Ma, I don't seem to be able to control myself.'

Tota saw her mother and asked, 'What's wrong, Ma, why are you crying?'

Anamitra was the one who answered. 'Your father has died, Tota, that's why she's crying.' Then she went to her room, leaving Tota puzzled.

# 2

Anamitra had achieved what she wanted to. When Siddhartha returned home and heard what had happened, he grew pale and avoided his mother. Mou left early the next morning with her children and belongings. Sanatan and his wife wanted to take the 11 a.m. bus, so they packed and came to offer their respects to Anamitra. She told them testily, 'Don't you know that you shouldn't be touching anyone's feet at this time?'

'Take care of Ma, Bou-di,' Sanatan said and left quickly. Anamitra was no less frustrated with Sanatan. Not only had he begun living here, he even kept telling her, 'There are very few people who are as generous as Ma. She treats a stranger with as much care as her own people.'

It didn't take long for the house to be cleared out. Only Tota remained. But she too informed them that she would leave in two days—she was just waiting to get her tickets confirmed. Anamitra's suspicions were proved right when Tota told Siddhartha, 'Dada, I was expecting you to discuss this, but you never even raised the subject. You know Baba left a will with Jyoti Kaka. I'd like it to be opened and read before I leave. Kaka will read it in your, my, and Ma's presence. I want to take all of my movable inheritance with me now. Truly, you could know a person for years and never find out what they're really like. I hadn't imagined in my worst nightmares that I'd have to see this side of Bou-di's character. I'm leaving Ma with you. Baba is gone, and Ma's fate is doomed anyway, so it looks like she'll have to spend the rest of her life enduring Bou-di's abuse. I'm not as free-spirited as your wife, I have to obey my in-laws. If I were as independent, maybe I would have taken Ma with me.'

Siddhartha began to scratch his beard as he listened to his younger sister lecture him. He didn't interrupt her. Then he said, 'All right, let's call Jyoti Kaka over tomorrow. But I'm warning you, Tota, you cannot remove a single piece from Baba's collection. I'm telling you this very clearly, I am not giving them to you. We cannot divide up Baba's prized possessions. He put that collection together over his lifetime, and it must be kept exactly how it's always been kept in his room.'

Tota lost her cool and began arguing loudly. Siddhartha flared up as well. Anamitra didn't interfere. She noticed that Ma didn't come out of her room to find out what was happening.

The next day, Jyoti Kaka read the will out to them. It wasn't so much an official will as an informal record of Baba's wishes. Besides Jyoti Kaka, the others present in the room were Asha, Tota, Siddhartha, and Anamitra.

Anamitra was shocked by her father-in-law's will. He had left Tota a great deal—money, jewellery, silver cutlery, shawls. But he had left Siddhartha the entirety of his prized collection. Anamitra felt relieved. She'd have been heartbroken if Tota took the blue tea set with her. Her father-in-law hadn't left his widow any material property. Siddhartha was to take care of her. Anamitra noted that she was barely listening to what Jyoti Kaka was reading out. At night, when Anamitra was turning off the lights in the long veranda before going to bed, her mother-in-law called out to her and put the keys to the larder in her hands. 'Perhaps you were right, Bou-ma. I think I never learnt to understand your father as a person beyond this household. And I think he never understood me beyond it either.'

# 3

Several months passed. Hardly anyone came to the house now. The hired priest hastily completed the evening puja in the thakurdalan and left. Anamitra's mother-in-law had grown very quiet. She spent most of her time in her own room. Her physical health had deteriorated quite suddenly. Climbing the stairs left her out of breath, so she was moved into the room beside the living room on the second floor. The room was right opposite Anamitra's. The kitchen and dining space used to be on the first floor with the room for cooking the sacred bhog, the prayer room, and the servants' quarters. Asha used to live on the third floor, and Siddhartha and Anamitra on the second floor. For her convenience, Siddhartha had the two rooms to the west remodelled into a kitchen and dining area, in accordance with the plan Anamitra had drawn up. Her mother-in-law emerged from her room only when meals were served. She no longer directed the affairs of the household. She didn't remind Anamitra of Ekadoshi, Purnima, or Ambubachi, or on what date the Bipodtarini Puja was to be conducted. To ensure she didn't make a mistake, Anamitra kept calling her own mother to ask, 'Ma, do remind me sometimes. I don't know how to read almanacs.'

Asha had grown so quiet that Siddhartha got irritated with Anamitra. 'What did you tell Ma that's made her stop being a part of anything? She doesn't even show any interest in her gods and stuff anymore. She's completely withdrawn into herself.'

Anamitra felt a little guilty. Tota didn't speak much with them either. She rang once every two or three weeks to check on her mother and hung up after a few minutes. To defend herself, Anamitra told Siddhartha, 'I don't remember what I said anymore, but I wasn't too rude. You were floundering to keep this household afloat. Do you realise now how much money you were wasting doing things the way Ma wanted? Look, Baba did trust you to look after Ma, and we haven't failed him. No one can accuse us of not treating her well. We cook what she likes to eat, she has a physiotherapist and a doctor, and I give her medication according to her schedule. We fulfil every responsibility children have towards their aged parents.'

'But the doctor says that it's Ma's depression that's making her sick. She's used to living her life a certain way, and giving up the reins to someone else has killed her spirit. That's what's causing her depression. Why did you need to change everything so soon? You could have done it slowly. My aunts used to come over all the time, they've completely stopped now. And Ma doesn't talk to us anyway.'

Anamitra flared up. 'All right then, I'll arrange for the carnival to start again. We'll feed 14 people day and night and call the weaver to give expensive zari saris to everyone for Itu Puja. What else did she do last time? Oh yes, she got 28 nose rings made because she wanted to give everyone some gold. Let's start all of that again, shall we? I'll throw myself at her feet and tell her, "Ma, please forgive me, please run your household the way you want." Ever since I've come to this house, I haven't had a single afternoon to myself to rest. Someone or the other always turns up and goes, "How are you Bou-ma," and keeps chattering. But now that I finally have some peace, you can't take it, can you?'

Siddhartha was silent for some time. Then he said, 'No, let it be. You don't need to say anything.'

'Listen, everyone has to retire at some point. Everyone has to give up. How is it my fault if your mother is sulking like a child? Can she not just depend on us for once? Are we really that terrible?'

# 4

The years passed. Everyone got used to Asha's silence. Anamitra had let go of two former servants—they had both grown quite old. They'd have spent the rest of their lives working for Anamitra if she had kept them on. But while Anamitra had grown more hard-hearted and calculating with age, and their relatives whispered about what a shrew she'd become, she hadn't become unreasonable. She'd arranged for their Brahmin cooks to receive pensions. She bought Nimai Kaka a plot of land and gave him money to build a house. Now, they only had two full-time servants. The constant clamour in the house was a thing of the past. Anamitra had a lot of leisure. She loved reading books but didn't watch television as much. She borrowed books from the library and brought them home to read.

Anamitra had managed to get rid of her mother-in-law's obsession with the household in a week. She had imprisoned and clipped the wings of a woman who delighted in living in a lively household, although she hadn't expected it to have quite this impact. Not only did her mother-in-law stay out of household affairs, she barely even opened her mouth to speak. But something kept bothering Anamitra. There was so much to see all around—the garden behind their house, the television. And yet, her mother-in-law forced her sleepy eyes open and kept staring through a door inside the house.

Asha's bed was right opposite the door. Whenever Anamitra passed it on the way from the kitchen to the living room, or from there to her room, or from her room to the balcony, she always saw her mother-in-law staring. This staring became so unbearable that Anamitra felt she had to do something about it. But she could no longer complain about things to Siddhartha, and this wasn't something one could really complain about in any case. She could almost hear Siddhartha telling her, 'You've taken everything away from Ma. Aren't you satisfied yet? Perhaps I should blind her in both eyes for your sake?'

She didn't bring it up with Siddhartha, and wondered if they should have installed her mother-in-law on the third floor. Finally, on a day when Siddhartha wasn't home, Anamitra shut the doors of her mother-in-law's room. Her mother-in-law didn't protest at this, didn't even call out for anyone. Shutting the door gave Anamitra some peace of mind, but whenever she entered the room for some reason, she found her mother-in-law lying in bed, staring unblinkingly at the door. Irritated, she asked, 'Doesn't your neck hurt, Ma? Don't your eyes hurt from staring all the time? Why do you keep looking at the door?'

Her mother-in-law said, 'But I don't.'

'Oh, don't you? Such nonsense!' Anamitra slammed the door shut again. But her unease never went away. She knew her mother-in-law was still staring in her direction. Her stare had pierced through the walls and doors and reached the heart of the household.